Bridging the Digital Divide

Divide

Social Media for Seniors

Table of Contents

The Internet, in general, and smartphones, in particular, are among the most important ways people seek and share health information. Seniors are going online, embracing social media, and their numbers will only grow.

— Susannah Fox

Chapter 1. Introduction

In our comprehensive Special Report titled "Bridging the Digital Divide: Social Media for Seniors," we uncover the myriad ways in which social media opens up a universe of connection, communication, and discovery for the older generation. With a simple touch or a click, the digital divide recedes, making way for an enriching, engaging, and exciting world that's all at your seniors fingertips. Presented in an easy-to-follow and jargon-free language, we provide insightful guidance and practical steps to help seniors harness the power of social media confidently and safely. Come aboard this digital journey, experience the pleasure of virtual camaraderie, and let's make the global community smaller, one click at a time! Your purchase of this Special Report not only encourages our work but also helps your loved ones navigate into the heart of the digital era with a reassuring sense of simplicity and fun!

Chapter 2. Understanding the Digital Divide: Its Causes and Effects

In this topical exploration of the 'Digital Divide', we embark on an analytical journey that scrutinizes the causes of this phenomena and its widespread effects across generations, with a particular spotlight on seniors. This chapter aims to establish a solid foundation of understanding before venturing into the labyrinth of social media.

2.1. Conceptualizing the Digital Divide

The term 'Digital Divide' is widely used to refer to the disparity in access to Information and Communication Technologies (ICT), including Internet and computer use, brought about by various socioeconomic factors. However simplistic this definition might seem, the concept runs a lot deeper, extrapolating into a universe of consequences and implications for an individual and society at large.

It's essential to remember that the 'Digital Divide' isn't merely concerned with who has a computer or internet access but more critically about the skills, knowledge, and confidence to aptly utilize these tools. Consequently, one might possess technological devices and even hold access to the web but still be haunted by the digital chasm.

2.2. Triggers of the Digital Divide

Deciphering the causes of the 'Digital Divide' warrants a dive into segregating factors like age, income, literacy levels, physical ability, and location. Let's dissect these one-by-one.

1. *Age*: Age stands as a paramount factor, primarily since technology's evolution pace often outstrips the older generation's comfort and adaptation speed. Akin to learning a new language, when exposed to the world of computers, smartphones, and the internet, seniors often feel like they're grappling with a foreign vocabulary and grammar.

2. *Income*: Lower-income groups often lack the financial means to procure the latest devices or afford reliable, high-speed internet, thereby widening the divide.

3. *Literacy Levels*: Illiteracy further drives the separation since comprehension and reciprocation become barriers in adopting and efficiently using digital technologies.

4. *Physical Ability*: Motor and sensory impairments such as weakened vision, hearing loss, or reduced dexterity can complicate interaction with digital devices and online interfaces.

5. *Location*: In areas marked with underdeveloped infrastructure or remote locales, accessing stable internet services may be a challenge in itself.

2.3. Consequences of the Digital Divide

A vast array of effects stem from the causes mentioned above and manifest in various life spheres for seniors.

1. *Social Isolation*: Detached from the digital world, seniors may experience a heightened sense of loneliness, given the increasing shift of communication and interaction to virtual platforms.

2. *Decreased Independence*: A lack of digital skills may result in seniors relying heavily on familial support for tasks like online shopping, banking, and health management, infringing on their

autonomy.

3. *Information Poverty*: Being disconnected digitally often translates to a dearth of ready-to-hand information, impacting decision-making, general awareness, and self-learning.

4. *Reduced Opportunities*: Career advancements, learning possibilities, and networking scenarios, all get curtailed when one exists outside the digital cosmos.

2.4. Bridging the Gap: A Glimpse Ahead

As we delve deeper into the chapters that follow, we shall explore how seniors can transcend the challenges that accompany the 'Digital Divide'. From setting up social media accounts to maintaining an active and safe online presence, this journey promises to imbue the learner with the confidence and skill set to stride credibly into the digital landscape.

Understanding the 'Digital Divide', its causes and effects, provides a crucial backdrop for this undertaking. It is with this knowledge that we gain sensitivity towards those grappling with this divide and garner the right perspective to promote inclusivity for seniors in the digital world.

Chapter 3. Social Media Basics: Platforms, Purposes, and Possibilities

The advent of social media has drastically changed the landscape of communication, offering a myriad of platforms each serving both similar and unique purposes. Each platform caters to diverse functionalities, varying from social networking, news dissemination, professional networking, knowledge sharing, to visual storytelling. Understanding the specifics of each social media service caters to can bring clarity and help seniors choose which ones suit their interaction and discovery needs the best.

3.1. Understanding the Purpose of Various Social Media Platforms

Let's embark on an exploration of the most popular social media platforms, their primary purposes, and how they can enrich your life.

1. **Facebook**: The most popular social media site globally, Facebook enables users to connect with friends and family regardless of geographic location. Here, you can share messages, post updates about your day, share photos, and join groups based on interests. There's plenty to enjoy, from reminiscing over a family photo album to participating in a gardening enthusiast group.

2. **Twitter**: This dynamic platform is a real-time stream of short messages ('tweets') from people, companies, and organizations you choose to follow. It is a great way to stay updated with current events, trends, and public discourse. Engage in lively discussions, or merely follow along with dynamic global

conversations.

3. **Instagram**: Owned by Facebook, Instagram is a photo and video sharing platform where users can capture, edit, and share their favourite moments visually. With its simple interface, Instagram is a perfect place for seniors to share their experiences or enjoy the beautiful imagery shared by others.

4. **LinkedIn**: A professional network platform where people connect with colleagues, find job opportunities and engage with industry-related content. Seniors can use LinkedIn to maintain professional connections, share their expertise, or even find part-time opportunities.

5. **Pinterest**: A unique platform where individuals can create and explore "boards" filled with images (or 'pins'). You can find inspiration for recipes, home decor, craft ideas, or any topic you could think of.

3.2. Getting to Know the Basic Features

After understanding their general purpose, it's important to familiarize yourself with the basic functionalities that most of these platforms have in common. Here's a brief rundown:

1. **Profile**: This is your digital representation on the platform. It typically contains your name, profile picture, and a short description.

2. **News Feed or Timeline**: This is where you'll see most of the content from individuals or groups you subscribe to, presented in a chronological stream.

3. **Likes/Reactions**: A simple way to show appreciation for a post or update, you can 'like' content across these platforms by clicking the like button, often represented by a heart or thumbs up icon.

4. **Comments**: If you want to articulate your thoughts beyond a simple reaction, you can leave a comment on a post. This is a space for conversation, questions, or sharing your thoughts.

5. **Sharing/Retweeting/Reposting**: If you find content that you'd like your own followers to see, you can share it on your own timeline. This function varies in name depending on the platform, but its core functionality remains the same.

6. **Messenger/Inbox**: Most platforms have a private messaging feature, where you can send direct messages to your connections. This is similar to email or text message, but within the social media platform.

3.3. Choosing the Right Platform for Senior Users

The choice of social media platform largely depends on personal needs and interests. If sharing photos and family updates is your primary goal, Facebook or Instagram might be suitable for you. For keeping up with breaking news and trend discussions, Twitter could be your go-to platform. LinkedIn is perfect for seniors who want to keep a finger on the pulse of their professional network and industry updates. And if you're looking for creative inspiration or a hub of ideas for various projects, Pinterest may pique your interest.

In conclusion, the world of social media is filled with diverse platforms offering an array of interaction opportunities. Understanding the basics will not only empower seniors to bridge the digital divide but will also open doors to an enriching online world of connections, shared interests, and engaging content. The next step is equally exciting - creating your own social media account, which we shall explore in the subsequent section. Your journey into harnessing the power of social media has only just begun!

Chapter 4. Setting Up Shop: A Guide to Creating Your Social Media Accounts

In the era of relentless digital proliferation, setting up social media accounts has become an essential routine for many, almost akin to a rite of passage into the digital community. This chapter serves as an expansive walkthrough guide to creating social media accounts. The contents stretch across the process from the ground up, covering all the vital steps from deciding the right platform to customizing your profile for a distinctive online identity.

4.1. Choosing the Right Platform

The first and quite possibly the most fundamental step your journey into the world of social media begins with is selecting the right platform. Social media platforms can range from the ephemerally personal, such as Snapchat, to the more professionally focused, like LinkedIn. The choice largely depends on what you want to gain from the platform - it might be reconnecting with old friends, staying informed about current events, or showcasing your hobbies and interests. Among the more popular platforms are Facebook, known for its comprehensive approach to social networking; Twitter, favored for real-time discussions and news; Instagram, perfect for sharing visual experiences; and LinkedIn, the go-to platform for professional networking. Spend time studying each platform, their offerings, and determine which best fits your needs.

4.2. Creating Your Account

Once you've decided on the platform to use, the next step is creating your account. While the steps may slightly differ per platform, the process typically involves inputting your personal information like full name and email address, and setting a secure password. It's crucial to use an active email account as most platforms verify your account via email.

For the password, consider using a combination of upper and lower case letters, numbers, and special characters. Remember, the complexity of your password often determines its strength.

4.3. Setting Up Your Profile

After your account is set up, it comes time to work on your profile, the digital representation of you on the platform. This typically consists of a profile picture, cover photo, and a short biography.

Your profile picture should be clear and ideally highlight your face. The cover photo, available on some platforms such as Facebook and Twitter, is often a larger image that can reflect your personality, interests, or milestones.

Your biography should briefly tell other users about you. It could contain your hobbies, profession, favorite quote, or anything that gives a snapshot into who you are.

4.4. Customising Privacy Settings

Now, just because you're on social media doesn't mean every aspect of your profile has to be public. Each platform offers varying degrees of privacy customization which you can adjust based on your comfort level. For example, you can choose who sees your posts, who can add you as a friend or follow you, and who can tag you in posts. Take time to navigate the privacy settings of your chosen platform to create a safe and comfortable environment for your online presence.

4.5. Connecting With Others

Once your account is set up, it's time to start making connections. Most platforms suggest friends or people to follow when you're new. These suggestions are based on the information you've provided, like your email address or phone number. Start small by adding people and organizations you know and trust. As you become more confident using the platform, you can expand your network further.

4.6. Posting Your First Status

Now comes the exciting part – publishing your inaugural post. This can be a simple text status, a photo, a link to an article, or even a video. Remember, the content you post contributes to the overall image of you on the platform. Choose something that reflects you, and is appropriate for the community you're joining.

In this digital age of connectivity, setting up a social media account doesn't have to be intimidating. With the right guidance and understanding, it can be an exciting doorway to new connections, insights, and experiences. This chapter aims to be your comprehensive guide, simplifying the process and offering practical suggestions to make your voyage into the social networking sphere effortless and enjoyable.

Chapter 5. Staying Safe Online: Essential Cybersecurity Tips for Seniors

The world of social media, while delightful in manifold ways, does bring with it certain risks. The digital universe has its unsavory elements, and seniors especially must take extra precaution to shield themselves from such dangers. This chapter will provide an in-depth analysis of the essential cybersecurity tips for seniors, helping ensure a safe, enjoyable, and fruitful excursion into the thrilling world of social media.

5.1. Understanding the Landscape: The Threats You Face Online

Just as in the physical world, understanding the landscape and its inherent risks is the first step to staying safe. The online universe, for all its benefits, is fraught with various types of threats including malware, phishing scams, online frauds, identity theft, and cyberstalking, to list just a few. Interpersonal communication, usually through interactively connected platforms known as social media, is a haven for cyber malefactors due to its openness and extensiveness. Hence, this makes it necessary to identify and understand these cyber threats before setting foot into the vast geography of the digital world.

5.2. A Strong Defense: Creating Secure Passwords

The central key to your online identity is your password. Far too often, individuals opt for simple, memorable passwords, which serve as weak barriers against online villains. Strong, unique passwords are fundamental shields you need in your defense arsenal. It might seem like a daunting task to remember complex passwords initially, but password managers can greatly help to lessen this burden. These digital lockboxes keep your passwords secure, and only require you to remember one main password. Rotating passwords periodically is also a good practice.

5.3. The Power of Two: Two-Factor Authentication

Two-factor authentication is akin to having a double lock on your door. It amalgamates something you know (your password) and something you have (a one-time code sent to your phone or email). This double barrier significantly boosts your online security and keeps would-be attackers at bay. Most social media platforms provide the option for this enabling feature. Leverage its power to augment your online safety.

5.4. Oversharing is Overbearing: Restricting What You Share

The thirst for sharing on social sites is extraordinarily cosmetic, but a grain of caution must be added here. Oversharing personal information can expose you to a host of cybersecurity threats. It is best to share minimal details and set your privacy settings to limit who can view what you share. Be intentional about the details you disclose on your social profiles and keep your online social circles restricted to known individuals and organizations.

5.5. Don't Fall for the Bait: Recognizing Scams and Phishing Attempts

Social media platforms are rife with scams and con artists attempting to trick users into revealing sensitive information or to make fraudulent transactions. Distinguish between legitimate businesses/individuals and dubious ones. Always make the extra effort to authenticate the identity of anyone requesting personal or financial information.

5.6. Keep Updated: Regularly Updating Software and Applications

Security vulnerabilities often stem from outdated software or applications. Updating your social media apps, along with the operating software, will ensure you are shielded from any known weak spots that may be exploited. A habit of downloading and installing updates at their earliest availability will reduce the risk of cyber threats.

5.7. Healthy Skepticism: Trusting Your Instincts Online

Just like real-life, skepticism could serve you well in the digital world. When it comes to social media, if anything appears fishy, it probably is. Be always on alert and never overlook any suspicions or uncertainties that you may feel while navigating social media.

In summary, as a senior user of social media, it is crucial to familiarize yourself with the cyber landscape, its threats, and the means to safeguard against them. The proper knowledge, coupled with carefulness can ensure you enjoy the plenitude of social media benefits without compromising your security and peace of mind. Embrace technology, but remember to do it responsibly and with a clear understanding of the online world's security demands. It isn't as intimidating as it may sound, and strategies like the ones above can guide you to become more cyber secure and thus enjoy the voyage into the universe of social media boldly and without trepidation.

Chapter 6. Building Your Network: Connecting with Friends, Family, and Interests

At the heart of our engagement with the pulsating world of social media is the ability to forge connections. With a broad selection of platforms that are readily available, you are not only privy to a colossal collection of content but can also craft your own network of contacts. This network can span friends and family, shared interests, causes, celebrities, institutions, and other entities that may pique your interest.

6.1. The Purpose of Building a Network

Understanding why you want to build a network on social media will help guide you in the right direction. For some, the primary motive may be to stay in touch with family and friends who could be geographically dispersed. Social media offers an incredibly accessible avenue to feel closer to your loved ones, see what they are up to, and interact with them on a routine basis, irrespective of physical distance. Others might wish to use these platforms to reconnect with contacts from their past, reigniting old friendships.

Further, you may want to follow organizations, causes, or individuals that resonate with your interests or passions, broadening your horizons and keeping abreast of the latest news and trends in fields of your choice. Essentially, your interests can serve as a beacon, compelling you to connect with like-minded individuals or communities across the globe, thereby enriching your social media experience.

6.2. Your First Steps in Building a Network

The first step in the process is to identify the people you already know on these platforms. Most social media sites have features allowing you to 'find friends' by importing contacts from your email account. Be selective about whom you choose to connect with. As a rule of thumb, if you wouldn't stop to chat with them on the street, it's probably not worth adding them to your online network.

6.3. Diversifying Your Network

While family members and friends form the atomic building blocks, there is an adventurous edge to exploring beyond your current sphere. You could start by following accounts, pages, or groups dedicated to topics that fascinate you. This could be anything from cooking and gardening to travel and photography, or even a hobby as specific as bird-watching or stargazing.

Joining themed groups can be another excellent way of diversifying your network. Communities on social media platforms often host debates and discussions, guaranteeing enriching interaction. It also proffers an opportunity to meet people who share your interests.

6.4. Nurturing and Growing Your Network

Cultivating your social media network involves more than solely clicking on the 'add friend' or 'follow' button. Engage by reacting to posts, leaving comments or even sharing posts that you find interesting. This two-way interaction encourages dialogue and fosters relationships.

As you become more accustomed to the social media landscape, you will discover that you can fine-tune your feed, prioritizing people, pages, or groups that you find most engaging, and muting or unfollowing those that don't enrich your online experience.

6.5. The Power of Mutual Connections

Another striking feature of the digitally woven network is the capacity to expand your connections using common friends or shared interests. Once you build your contact list and start interacting with different users, your network's potential to grow further becomes exponential. This creates a sort of ripple effect, where engaging with one connection could lead you to others.

6.6. Treading with Caution: Protecting Your Privacy

Nevertheless, in your digital networking journey, it is essential to tread cautiously and protect your privacy. This involves careful contemplation about the type of information you divulge about yourself, continually reviewing and managing your privacy settings, blocking or reporting any untoward behavior, and treating digital interactions with the same level of discernment as real-life relationships.

Social media is a space for expression and connection. Approach it with curiosity and caution, enjoying the myriad possibilities it presents while retaining control over your online footprint. Happy networking!

Chapter 7. Facebook for Seniors: Tips, Tricks, and Everyday Use

The popularity of Facebook is universally acknowledged, stretching across various generations. It's not just a space reserved for the young, and with the right guidance, it's an engaging platform that seniors can master, too. This chapter intends to break down the complex, unravel the seemingly complicated, and make Facebook not just senior-friendly but also senior-liked. We will explore a myriad of features that Facebook offers, including how to create an account, customize your profile, connect with others, ensure privacy, and use Facebook apps to their fullest potential.

7.1. Understanding Your Facebook Profile

The first step on this Facebook journey is to set up an account. But worry not; the process is straightforward. First, head on over to the Facebook homepage on your internet browser, and you'll see a "Create New Account" option on the right-hand side of the screen. Click on it and follow the simple instructions to set up your account. Merely input your details, including your full name, birthdate, and contact information, and tailor a safe and secure password for your account. Once this is done, you have officially crossed the threshold into the Facebook universe!

Now, let's tackle the Facebook Profile. This is your personal page, a mirror reflecting your personality, interests, and life events to those who visit. You can customize it with profile and cover photos. The profile photo, perhaps a smiling headshot of you, is the main image that represents you on Facebook. The cover photo is the large banner at the top of your profile page which can be a reflection of your personality, a stylized picture of your pet, a scenic shot from your favorite location, or anything else that pleases you. You can also share a mini biography about yourself in the "About" section. Share as much or as little as you feel comfortable with, but remember, this information is accessible by those whom you allow in your network.

7.2. Finding Connections & Building Your Network

Once you have set up your profile, the next step is to start connecting with friends, family members, and groups that align with your interests. Type their names into the search bar on top of the screen, and when you find them, click on the 'Add Friend' button on their profile. You can also accept friend requests by clicking 'Confirm' when someone sends you a request.

Facebook Groups are another exciting aspect of building your network. Groups are specialized sections on Facebook where individuals with shared interests can connect, share, and engage with relevant content. You can join groups such as book clubs, travel enthusiasts, gardening gurus, or senior advice panels by typing the keywords into the search bar, clicking 'Groups', and then 'Join'.

7.3. Navigating through the News Feed

Your News Feed is essentially your Facebook homepage and is the first thing you see when you log in. Here, you'll find posts from your friends, liked pages, and joined groups—ranging from status updates to images, videos, and much more.

Learning to interact with posts is essential. Below each post, there are options for you to 'Like', 'Comment', or 'Share'. Feel free to engage as suits you - a kind 'Like' to your grandchild's achievement post, a heartfelt comment on your old friend's reunion photo, or sharing an enlightening article from a favored group.

7.4. Ensuring Privacy and Security

Navigating Facebook's privacy settings may seem daunting initially, but it is crucial to guarantee your security. From the "Settings & Privacy" page, you could control who sees your posts, who can send you friend requests, and even block people when necessary. You have several options for audience selection–from 'Public', which means everyone on Facebook can see, to 'Only Me', which means only you can view.

Remember to often update your password and use different passwords for different platforms. Facebook also offers two-factor authentication for added security. This feature requires both your password and a special code (usually sent to your mobile device) to log in.

7.5. Exploring Facebook Apps

Did you know that Facebook has a family of apps that can further enrich your user experience? Messenger, for example, allows private communication with your Facebook friends. You can send messages, make voice and video calls, and even share images and videos privately.

Industry experts project that Facebook's older-user demographics will continue growing as more seniors join the platform, making it an essential tool for seniors to stay active, engaged, and socially connected. With these tips and tricks, you can make everyday use of this platform an enjoyable part of your daily routine. Remember that while it's essential to have fun and connect with those dear to you, it's equally important to safeguard your online privacy and maintain a healthy digital lifestyle. Happy Facebook-ing!

Chapter 8. Twitter for Seniors: Following Conversations and Trends

Twitter is a social media platform where people share thoughts, information, and news in real time. While it may seem intimidating at first, with a little patience and practice, you'll find it to be an excellent tool for staying updated on news, events, and trending topics.

8.1. Setting Up Your Twitter Account

Before you can immerse yourself in the world of tweets and hashtags, the first step is to set up a Twitter account. This involves choosing a username (or handle), uploading a profile picture, crafting a brief personal bio, and selecting your interests.

1. Visit www.twitter.com and click on the 'Sign Up' button.

2. Provide your name and phone number or email address. You'll receive a verification code to continue the process.

3. Choose a unique handle. This is your identity on Twitter, prefaced by the @ symbol.

4. Pick a tasteful, clear profile picture and write a succinct bio that encapsulates who you are or what you're interested in.

5. Select your areas of interest. Twitter will then suggest accounts to follow relevant to those interests.

Once you complete these steps, your Twitter account is ready for use!

8.2. Navigating the Twitter Interface

Twitter's interface can initially appear somewhat complex, particularly with the constant stream of tweets updated in real-time. However, understanding the fundamental components can simplify this.

1. Home: This is your personal feed where tweets from accounts you follow will appear.

2. Explore: Discover what's trending on Twitter globally or locally. You can find news, events, viral hashtags, and more.

3. Notifications: Here, you'll see who has followed you, liked or retweeted your tweets, and mentioned you in their tweets.

4. Messages: This is where your private direct messages (DMs) are stored.

5. Profile: View your tweets, who you're following, and your followers here.

8.3. Tweeting, Retweeting, and Replying

Now that you can navigate Twitter, let's explore how to interact on the platform. Remember, tweets have a maximum of 280 characters.

To compose a tweet, click on the quill icon or the 'Tweet' button, write your message, and select 'Tweet'. Express your thoughts, share an interesting link, or post a beautiful photo - the choice is yours!

You can also interact with other people's tweets. Click the heart icon to 'like' a tweet, or press the rotate symbol to 'retweet' and share that message with your followers. To reply, click on the speech bubble and type your response.

8.4. Discovering and Following Trends

One of Twitter's best features is its ability to highlight 'trending' topics - these could be news headlines, popular hashtags, or viral stories. Visit the 'Explore' tab and immerse yourself in the topics that have Twitter buzzing.

You can follow trends not just globally, but also within specific geographical areas. This is particularly exciting if you want to stay abreast with local news, events, or stories.

Remember, selecting and following trends that align with your interests will drastically improve your Twitter experience.

8.5. Following Accounts and Building your Network

Following accounts whose tweets you find interesting is a crucial aspect of your Twitter journey. They could be family, friends, celebrities, news outlets, organizations, or thought leaders. As you follow more accounts, your Twitter feed will become richer with diverse perspectives and insights.

Remember, Twitter, like any social platform, is about interaction and engagement. You can reach out to people, join conversations, and express your viewpoints.

8.6. Practicing Twitter Safety

As with all social media platforms, maintaining online safety necessitates caution. Be prudent about the personal information you share, and avoid any engagement that seems suspicious. Always use a strong, unique password and consider enabling two-factor authentication for an additional layer of security.

Also, remember that Twitter allows you to limit who can send you direct messages or reply to your tweets, offering control over your interactions.

Twitter holds immense potential for enriching your digital life. It offers real-time connection to global conversations, news, and trends. It may feel overwhelming initially, but remember, as with any new skill, mastery comes with practice. Happy tweeting!

Chapter 9. Instagram for Seniors: Documenting and Sharing Your Life

The concept of Instagram might appear bewildering at first glance for those unacquainted with it. But worry not; this chapter aims to break down the challenges and curiosities, offering an immersive guide through this visual-focused platform. You'll soon discover how Instagram can be an enjoyable way to document and share your life, connecting with loved ones, friends, and even the world at large.

9.1. What is Instagram and Why Should Seniors Use It?

Instagram is an innovative social media platform that focuses on the sharing and exploration of photos and videos. Users post pictures of their daily lives, travel experiences, culinary creations, gardening projects, and much more. Instagram thus becomes a digital photo album, interwoven with snippets of your life as well as the lives of those you follow.

Why should seniors use Instagram, you may ask? Firstly, Instagram allows you to gain insight into the ebbs and flows of your loved ones' lives. Secondly, it becomes a conduit to stimulate memories and foster connections through shared visuals. For those with hobbies or interests – say gardening, painting, or even bird-watching – Instagram enables the discovery of a whole universe of like-minded enthusiasts.

9.2. Setting Up Your Instagram Account

Before delving into the Instagram universe, you first need an account. Open your App Store (for iOS users) or Google Play Store (for Android users) and download the Instagram app. Tap the Instagram icon to open the app, then follow the prompts - enter your email, create a username and password, and fill in your profile details. Make sure to create a strong password for optimal security. Once you have set all these up, you are ready to start your Instagram journey.

9.3. Navigating the Instagram Interface

The Instagram interface, though seemingly complex, can be broken down into five main components:

1. Home: An endless feed of photos and videos from people you follow.

2. Search and Explore: Allows you to search for other Instagram users, hashtags, or places.

3. Camera: Enables you to take photos or record videos directly within the app.

4. Activity: Reveals 'likes', comments, and new followers you've garnered.

5. Profile: Your personal space displaying your posts, followers, and who you're following.

Familiarize yourself with these features; with time, navigation will be smooth and effortless.

9.4. Posting Pictures and Videos: Your First Instagram Post

When you're ready to share, tap the '+' icon at the bottom center of your screen. You have several options: choose a pre-existing photo or video from your library, capture a new photo, or record a fresh video. Once you've selected or taken your desired picture or video, tap 'Next'. This step leads you to an array of filters to enhance your image - a defining characteristic of Instagram. Once satisfied, tap 'Next' again to move to the caption screen. Here you can write a description of your post, add relevant hashtags, and tag fellow Instagram users if desired. Tap 'Share' to publish your post - and voila! You've made your first Instagram post.

9.5. Interacting with Other Users and Exploring Content

You can follow other users on Instagram, from family to friends, celebrities to hobby-based accounts. This process adds their posts to your home feed, effectively creating a community tailored to your interests. Interactions ensue through 'liking' posts (double-tap on a picture) or leaving comments (tap the speech bubble icon).

Moreover, the 'Explore' feature serves curated content based on your interests, introducing you to various users, trends, and topics.

9.6. Staying Safe on Instagram: Privacy and Interactions

As with any digital platform, understanding privacy settings on Instagram is critical. To ensure your account is private, navigate to 'Settings', then 'Privacy', and select 'Account Privacy'. Toggle the switch to ensure only those you approve can see your posts.

Remember, polite and respectful interactions foster a positive networking environment. Avoid sharing too much personal information, and report any unwelcome interaction or content.

9.7. Instagram Stories and Live Video Features

Instagram Stories allow you to share photos or videos that disappear after 24 hours. This feature is perfect for less permanent moments you wish to share. To create a story, tap the camera icon or swipe right from anywhere in Feed. Tap capture to take a photo, or hold to record a video.

For a more interactive experience, Instagram Live allows you to live-stream videos and interact with viewers in real-time. To start a live video, swipe right from your Feed. Tap 'Live' at the bottom, then tap 'Start Live Video'.

Instagram, with its blend of multimedia, interactive features, and simplicity, has the power to transform digital engagement amongst seniors. It offers avenues to share moments, connect with loved ones, revisit past memories, and even make new friends. Through careful navigation and mindful use, Instagram can indeed be a delightful extension of your life's journey shared with the world. Welcome to the Instagram community, where the world is just a snapshot away!

Chapter 10. LinkedIn for Lifelong Learners: Building Networks and Sharing Skills

As we tread the path of digital learning, the versatile platform called LinkedIn emerges as a unique networking tool for our exploration. For seniors eager to dive into the knowledge pool, its benefits are manifold. LinkedIn empowers lifelong learning with its networking capabilities, job opportunities, and skill-sharing features that keenly resonate with seniors. It opens the door to a vast library of knowledge, enables the sharing of insights and experiences, and facilitates connections with experts and peers alike.

10.1. Creating Your LinkedIn Profile

Your first encounter with LinkedIn is through your profile creation process, a true virtual representation of you. Begin by uploading a professional headshot, portraying you in a confident and approachable light. Then, craft a succinct yet impressionable headline, summarizing your skills or professional expertise.

Step into the 'About' section with the commitment to represent your unique story compellingly. Share your experience, ambitions, and skills with a tone of authenticity and conviction. The Experience and Education sections blueprint your journey, an opportunity to present a detailed chronicle of your past roles, responsibilities, projects, and learning journey.

Use the 'Licenses & Certifications' section if you have acquired certificates from online courses. Remember to add skills in the 'Skills & Endorsements' section, integral for fellow networkers to understand your capabilities, and for the LinkedIn algorithm to curate relevant content. Replace list items here with the skills relevant to you.

- Coding
- Digital Marketing
- Leadership
- Project Management
- Public Speaking

Include your contact information, and you're set with a competitive profile. Note that privacy settings are customizable to suit your comfort.

10.2. Networking on LinkedIn

Networking forms the essence of LinkedIn experience. Start by connecting with people you know personally, like family, friends, and former colleagues. Post that, move on to connecting with professionals in fields of your interest, engage with their content, contribute to discussions, thereby expanding your network horizon.

LinkedIn Groups vitiate an enriching space to delve deeper into specific domains. Look for groups that align with your interests, contribute to discussions, and you could stumble upon invaluable connections.

Engaging with posts, commenting and sharing insights play a pivotal role in nurturing network relationships. Remember, networking is a two-way street pivoted on mutual interactions.

10.3. Learning and Skill Sharing on LinkedIn

LinkedIn Learning offers a suite of courses across diverse domains, from technology to humanities. Utilize this feature, particularly effective for seniors wishing to hone new skills or brush up old ones.

Sharing your unique expertise is as crucial as acquiring new ones. Write articles, create posts, or share valuable resources relating to your skills and knowledge. This not only piques the interest of your network, but also reflects your active engagement in the field, enhancing your digital presence on the platform.

10.4. Ensuring Safety on LinkedIn

Your security on LinkedIn should always be a priority. Regularly review your privacy settings, keep your connections genuine, avoid sharing sensitive information, and report suspicious activities swiftly. Staying vigilant will help you steer clear of scams or breaches.

In summary, LinkedIn is a gold mine for seniors active in the lifelong learning journey. Its potential extends beyond job search and stands testament to the saying - 'You're never too old to learn'. The global classroom is buzzing with knowledge exchange, and it's your turn to step in and reap its benefits.

Chapter 11. The Future of Senior Digital Engagement: What's Next in Social Media

In the rapidly evolving landscape of digital technologies, social media stands tall as the frontier for inclusive communication. It transcends borders, binding hearts and minds in a shared, digital community. In recent years, seniors have been joining this global community, daring to cross the imposing digital divide. The journey has been empowering, empowering both their daily experiences and interactions. As the curtain rises on a future bright with digital possibilities, we delve into what's next in social media for senior engagement, exploring new technologies, platforms, and trends.

11.1. The Rise of Augmented Reality and Virtual Reality

With economies and societies advancing in volatility, uncertainty, complexity, and ambiguity, augmented reality (AR) and virtual reality (VR) are emerging as powerful social media tools. They provide immersive experiences, allowing seniors to virtually 'step into' different worlds, activities or events. Despite the relatively nascent stage of VR and AR, we're starting to see them used in applications beyond gaming. For instance, Facebook launched Horizon, a sprawling, VR world for users to explore, create, and connect in 3D. Instagram, on the other hand, has been utilizing AR for face filters.

An implication for seniors is that they can participate in events or visits that they're physically unable to attend. They could take a virtual tour to a historical monument halfway around the globe or attend a grandchild's wedding ceremony from the comfort of their homes. This need not be a solitary experience either, as multiplayer options allow real-time interaction with friends and family in the virtual space.

While it's fair to be wary of AR and VR's complexities, it is also worth appreciating the potential. Guides and tutorials tailored for seniors can help ease the learning process. In the coming days, we foresee user-friendly integrations in social media platforms to make adoption simpler, transforming the boundaries of connection and experience for our senior community!

11.2. The Advancement of Artificial Intelligence

Artificial intelligence (AI) is another technological marvel making steady inroads into our digital lives. AI-backed algorithms play a critical role in presenting curated content to social media users based on their preferences, interactions, and search history. Emerging AI functionality could help seniors navigate online spaces more efficiently.

For example, AI can guess and auto-correct typos, suggest words or phrases, and even convert speech to text. Furthermore, AI-powered chatbots can assist seniors in learning how to use social media features or answer queries— providing 24/7 on-demand support. And with advancing facial recognition technologies, AI can help seniors easily tag friends and family in their photos.

While AI's implications are vast and transformative, it is essential to be aware of privacy considerations too. The trade-off between personalization and privacy is a significant concern as AI algorithms often require a large amount of personal information to function efficiently. Understanding these dynamics is vital as we continue further into the digital age.

11.3. The Growing Influence of Live Streaming

Live streaming has transformed into one of social media's most compelling features. YouTube, Facebook, and Instagram all offer live streaming options, allowing users to share real-time video content with their network. Seniors can participate in shared live experiences, major events, or simply enjoy moments with distant friends and family, fostering a sense of belongingness and connection.

In summary, as we march forward, diving deeper into this digital world, we need to remain critical consumers and informed users. The next decade will likely bring AR, VR, AI, and more into mainstream social media use. As seniors navigate this ever-evolving digital terrain, remembering the fundamental tenets of online safety is crucial. In parallel, we must foster an atmosphere of continuous learning and curiosity. After all, the beauty of the virtual world is in its fluidity and constant resurrection with innovations. Embracing this nature, harnessing its power, and doing so with informed responsibility will ensure that the digital divide continues to narrow, one senior and one click at a time.